What Are You Looking At?

Contents

Written by Clare Gittings

What is a portrait?

A portrait is a picture of someone, and it can be made of any material. It can be painted or drawn; it can be a photograph or a **collage**. It can even be made of clay or filmed as a video portrait. The person in a portrait is called a **sitter**, even if they are standing up or lying down.

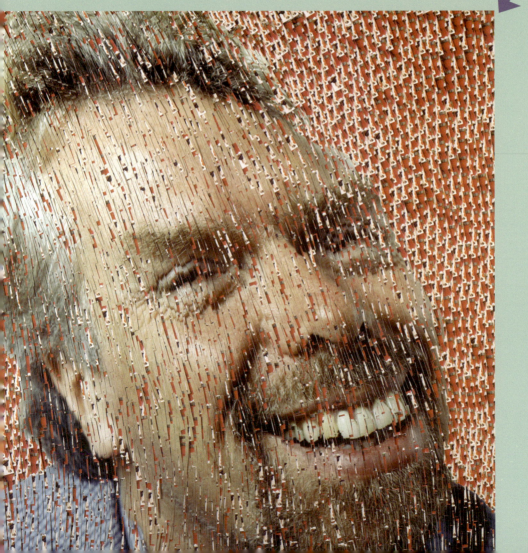

Richard Branson David Mach 1991. Made from a collage of postcards

Portraits are created for lots of reasons, as you will discover in this book. Susie Cooper was a potter so she chose clay to make this portrait of herself, because it was what she enjoyed working with.

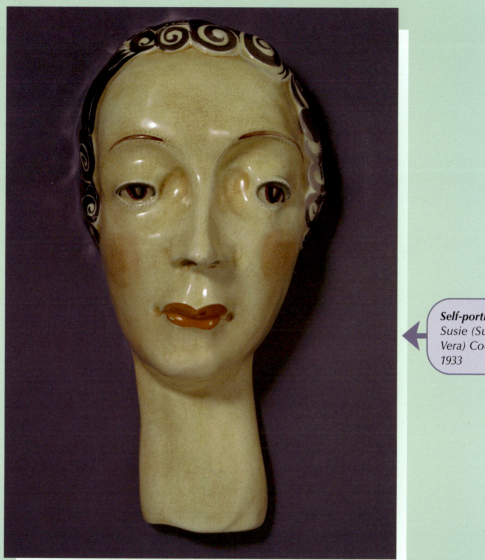

Self-portrait
Susie (Susan Vera) Cooper, 1933

Portraits can be different sizes depending on why the portrait was made. This is called the scale of the portrait.

Most of the portraits in this book are a great deal bigger than you see them here and some of them, like this life-size drawing of King Henry VIII, are huge. The artist, Hans Holbein, had to stick more than twenty pieces of paper together to make a big enough area to draw on.

King Henry VIII
Hans Holbein the
Younger, c. 1536-7

This drawing shows Henry VIII as tall as he was in real life. We know this because his armour is exactly this height. Hans Holbein used the drawing to help him create a **mural** of Henry VIII and his family on a wall in Henry's palace, and this part shows Henry with his father. The idea was that the finished life-size painting would be as impressive as seeing the king himself – it certainly amazed Tudor visitors who saw it.

This portrait of Queen Elizabeth I is so small it would fit into the palm of your hand. It is called a **miniature** and it's the same size in real life as it is on this page.

This is its actual size.

Queen Elizabeth I
Nicolas Hilliard, 1572

The portrait was painted in watercolour on animal skin and sometimes the artist mixed a little of his earwax into the paint to help it stick. The small black dot that you can see in each pearl is real silver, which has gone black with age. The artist made them shine by polishing the silver with a weasel's tooth.

Miniatures were often given as gifts and were worn round people's necks as jewellery.

Often, artists made sitters look better than they really were to please them and to make sure that they bought the portrait. Elizabeth was very interested in every detail of this portrait and she discussed it with Nicolas Hilliard, the artist.

Notice that she is wearing her favourite flower, a rose.

pieces of silver

Finding clues

Sitters have their portraits painted because they want to tell people about themselves, so artists put clues into the portraits that give messages about the sitters. Viewers need to find these clues and work out what they mean.

Christopher Anstey with daughter Mary William Hoare, c. 1776-8

One clue is the position of the sitter's body. This is called the **pose**, and in some portraits it can tell a whole story. Look at the man's pose and his daughter's as she tries to get his attention in this portrait.

The little girl is smiling, which is quite rare in painted portraits. It's hard to keep smiling long enough for the artist to paint the portrait – it begins to hurt. She's looking at her father, which leads our eyes to him. He's looking into the distance, thinking. Artists often put clues in the sitter's face, and you can tell a lot about someone from their **expression**. Do you think he minds being interrupted?

Anstey's daughter is pulling her father's jacket to get his attention.

Another clue to interpret is what the sitter is wearing. If you're going to be painted or photographed you usually put on your best clothes. However, here the comedian Gina Yashere has chosen to dress in jeans and a T-shirt, maybe deliberately, to look casual and relaxed. Another place to look for clues is in the **background**. Gina has chosen a public park, a place where everyone can go.

Gina Yashere
Sal Idriss, 2002

Notice the blurred edge of the umbrella.

Wearing casual clothes and being in an everyday place could have made Gina Yashere's portrait look very ordinary. However, she and the photographer have come up with the idea of her twirling her white umbrella. The blurred effect brings movement into the photograph and turns it into something unusual. The portrait makes Gina seem very approachable but is still exciting and distinctive.

Now look at this portrait of Viv Richards. You've probably already spotted that he's a cricketer. His pose shows that he has just hit the ball really hard and is still holding his cricket bat at the end of its stroke. He is watching the moving ball carefully with an expression of intense concentration on his face. The artist also plays cricket and said about this painting: "My interest is in the action."

You can tell that there's a huge crowd in the background watching the cricket match, but the style of painting makes the spectators look blurred and out of focus. This helps direct attention to Viv Richards, who is painted far more precisely. It is also how the crowd might appear to a batsman who is concentrating on playing cricket.

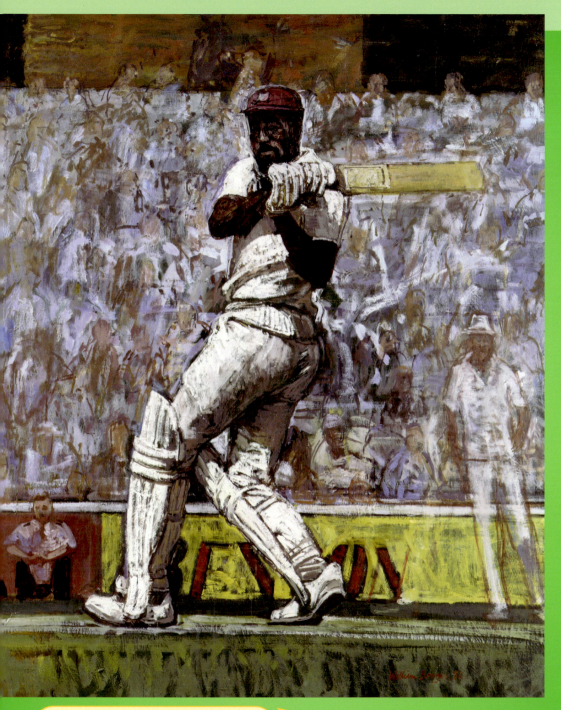

Sir Isaac Vivian Alexander (Viv) Richards
William Bowyer, 1986

Sarah Siddons
Sir William Beechey, 1793

Look carefully at this portrait. Sarah Siddons is holding a knife and looks like a murderer – but no murderer would really want to be painted like this. This is a portrait of a famous actress playing the part of a murderess, Lady Macbeth. Notice how the light falls on her to give a dramatic effect, just as stage lighting would.

stone showing Shakespeare's name

Sarah Siddons is acting in a play by Shakespeare and you can see his name carved in the stone beside her. She's holding a tragic mask with a turned down mouth, to show how skilled she is at playing tragic heroines. But her quiet smile suggests that in real life, she might be a very different kind of person.

Dorothy Hodgkin was a famous scientist and her work was very important to her. This is suggested by the way she is too busy even to look up at the painter. Notice the concentration on her face and the desk covered with papers.

Do portraits always tell the truth? Sometimes artists make changes to their sitters to tell you more about them. Dorothy Hodgkin has been painted with four hands to show how quickly she moves, just like in cartoons. You can also see that she was badly affected by **arthritis**, which made her hands look knobbly.

Look at the scientific model on her desk. This is a reminder that she was famous for winning the Nobel Prize for Chemistry.

Dorothy Mary Crowfoot Hodgkin
Maggi Hambling, 1985

Peter Blake is an artist who was interested in Pop Art in the 1960s, as was Clive Barker who made this collage of him. They both liked working with unusual materials and putting **puns** and jokes into their work. This is a collage that uses real objects as well as paint. The sitter's name is made by using tin openers to wind back the shapes of the letters in a sheet of copper metal.

Sir Peter Thomas Blake
Clive Barker, 1983

Peter Blake's hair is made of daisies because one of his daughters is called Daisy. His other daughter is called Liberty, so she is included through the two postage stamps showing the Statue of Liberty in New York.

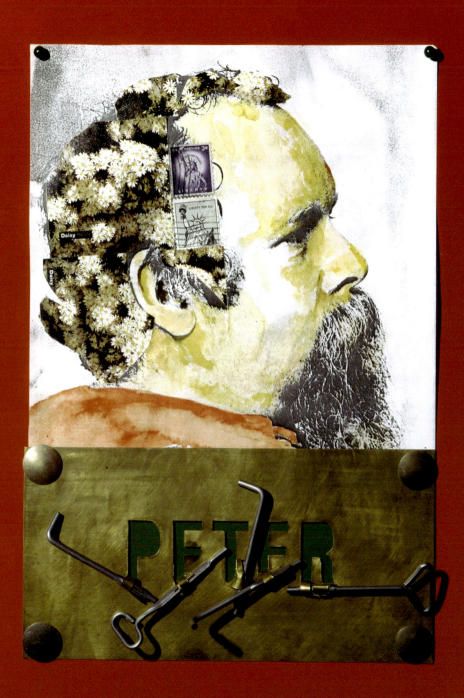

Animals in portraits

Portraits can also feature animals. This is Kitty Fisher who, with Lucy Locket, had a nursery rhyme made up about her that starts: "Lucy Locket lost her pocket, Kitty Fisher found it." Kitty Fisher was a real person, famous for her beauty. The artist painting her has chosen to use animals to put her name into the painting.

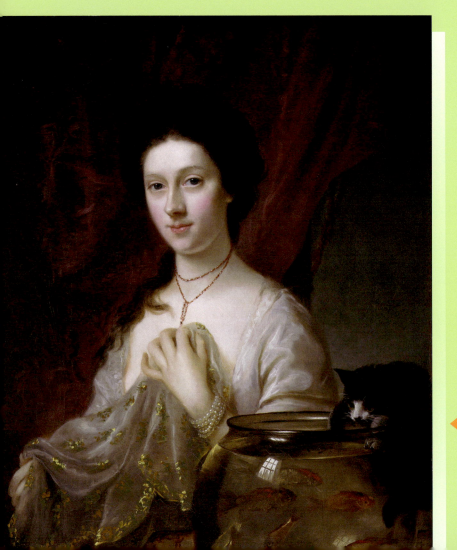

Kitty (Catherine Maria) Fisher Nathaniel Hone, 1765

The kitten is for "Kitty" and the fish are for "Fisher".

If you look carefully at the goldfish bowl you can see the reflection of a window with nine panes of glass. At the bottom of the window there are some people looking in at Kitty. The artist is showing you that she was such a celebrity that people were desperate to catch a glimpse of her.

This portrait shows Sir Edwin Landseer, who created the huge bronze lions in Trafalgar Square in London. He used the lion at London zoo as a model and had a real lion's skin in his studio. It's said that the lion in the zoo died before Landseer had finished his work and that his bronze lions' paws are really copied from a pet cat.

He was angry about this painting because his lions were meant to be a secret until they were actually installed in Trafalgar Square. When this portrait showing him at work was displayed, it gave the secret away.

The artist's dog is curled up near him, between the lion's paws. Maybe the painter wanted to make a joke that the little dog is taking no notice of the fact that it's asleep between the paws of a ferocious lion. It's also a way of reminding people that Sir Edwin was a famous Victorian painter of animals.

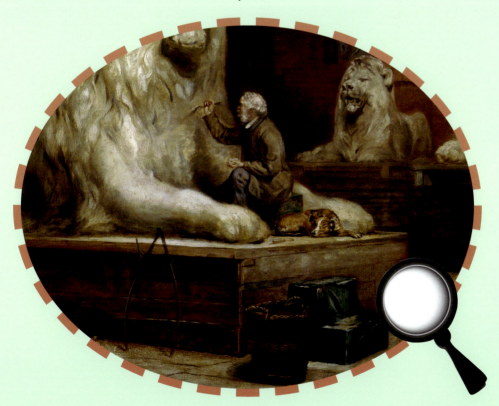

Self-portraits

If you make a portrait of yourself it's called a self-portrait. Artists use themselves as models to show what they look like and also how good their work is, almost like an advertisement, but they don't often make money from their self-portraits unless they're very famous. In their self-portraits artists sometimes try out new ideas and are more daring than when painting other people.

Self-portrait
*Angelica Kauffmann,
c. 1770-75*

Angelica Kauffman, in her self-portrait, has chosen to show herself drawing with a crayon rather than painting, even though she has actually painted this picture using oil paint. She may have done this because drawing is less messy than painting. She wanted to wear her best dress to prove how skilfully she could paint beautiful fabrics.

Self-portrait
John Tunnard, 1959

The artist John Tunnard wasn't only interested in painting, so he used his self-portrait to show what his other interests were. He loved nature and studied insects and seaweeds, so he created this strange image of his face as half man, half insect and added seaweed in the background.

26

You might not have immediately recognised this as a self-portrait. The artist Roland Penrose didn't start with what he looked like but with his name. He painted the word "Roland" in large capital letters and also in mirror writing. If you turn his self-portrait on its side you can just about read the letters. His eyes appear in the two letter Os.

Self-portrait
*Sir Roland Algernon Penrose,
c. 1948*

This self-portrait shows William Frith in his studio in London, sitting at his **easel**. The long stick he's holding is to keep his hand steady while painting. In his studio are brightly coloured clothes and **drapes** for dressing up a model.

Notice how the light streams into the picture onto the artist's face – but you can't see what he's painting. Also, you can only see part of the woman's face.

The woman who has come to model for him is dressed all in black so someone has just died, maybe her husband. Perhaps she's now so poor that she needs to be an **artist's model** to earn enough money to live. She is lifting her veil. Is this a way of showing that she's telling him about her life?

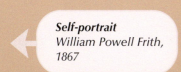

Self-portrait
William Powell Frith,
1867

Group portraits

Often a group portrait shows a family or people who work together and sometimes the artist is in the picture too. The most important sitters are usually in the middle or at the front of the group and the artist makes them stand out in some way. Perhaps light is falling on them, or perhaps the other sitters are looking towards them.

This portrait shows the Vyner family in their garden. The Vyners were a wealthy family who were painted in 1673. The father, Robert, is wearing what looks to us like a dressing gown, but rich men in those days wore gowns all day at home.

The family of Sir Robert Vyner (Bridget, Duchess of Leeds; Mary, Lady Vyner; Charles Vyner; Sir Robert Vyner) John Michael Wright, 1673

In this family there are two children. Charles, the boy in the middle, is the only child of Robert and his wife Mary, while Bridget is Mary's daughter from an earlier marriage. The artist has made Charles look important by painting the dog gazing up at him. The painter seems to be showing that Charles is allowed to do anything he wants.

You've already seen these lions on page 22 with their **sculptor**, Edwin Landseer. Here they are again, finished, in Trafalgar Square in London. You can also see Big Ben.

This group portrait is painted in a very different way from the portrait of the Vyners. The artist, Hans Schwarz, has chosen a popular public place as the background to show that the three men spent their lives helping the public, by fighting for better pay for working people.

The artist appears in the background of the painting, wearing a bright blue top, just beside a lion. Hans Schwartz liked painting with bright colours.

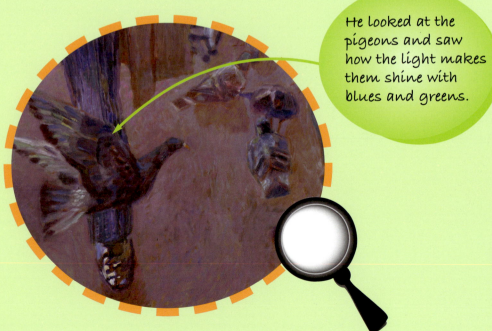

He looked at the pigeons and saw how the light makes them shine with blues and greens.

Trade Unionists (Joseph [Joe] Gormley, Baron Gromley; Thomas Jackson; Sidney Weighell)
Hans Schwarz, 1984

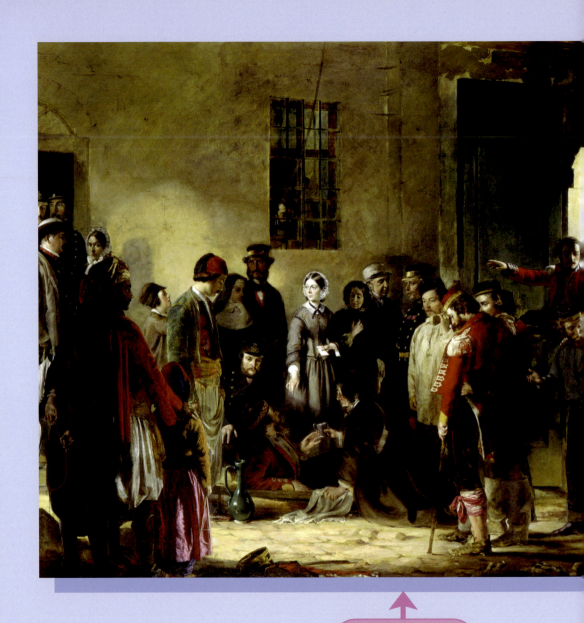

The Mission of Mercy:
Florence Nightingale
receiving the wounded
at Scutari
Jerry Barrett, 1857

This portrait is of Florence Nightingale. She went to the country that's now called Turkey, to nurse British soldiers wounded in the Crimean war. She was a national hero and the picture is very dramatic. Notice how light is streaming down on Florence, so you have no difficulty in spotting her. Her pose is very commanding.

The artist, Jerry Barrett, couldn't ask all these people to stop what they were doing and pose together, so he sketched Florence and her nurses at work in the hospital. He then painted a small **version** to try out his ideas before painting this big picture. The kneeling woman is Florence Nightingale's best nurse, Mrs Roberts, and he's careful that she doesn't take attention away from Florence.

Jerry Barrett also put himself in the picture. He's in the window, looking down at Florence. He read about Florence in the newspapers and went all the way to Turkey to make drawings of her, of the hospital and of the soldiers. He wants the viewer to know that he was really there.

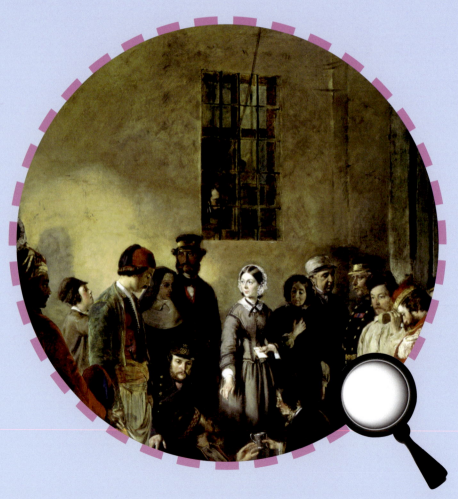

Jerry was proud of the fact that he painted from life and he included details to prove it. You can tell that it's hot because the dogs are lying down in the shade. He shows people in Turkish dress and in the distance you can see the **minarets** of the mosques. The wounded soldiers have arrived by boat from the battlefield and have to walk uphill to the hospital.

The dogs are on the ground.

Famous people

Mary Seacole was born in Kingston in the West Indies. Her mother was a healer. Mary followed in her footsteps and became a nurse. She wanted to work with Florence Nightingale, but Florence refused. However, Mary still went to Turkey, nursing wounded soldiers on the battlefield.

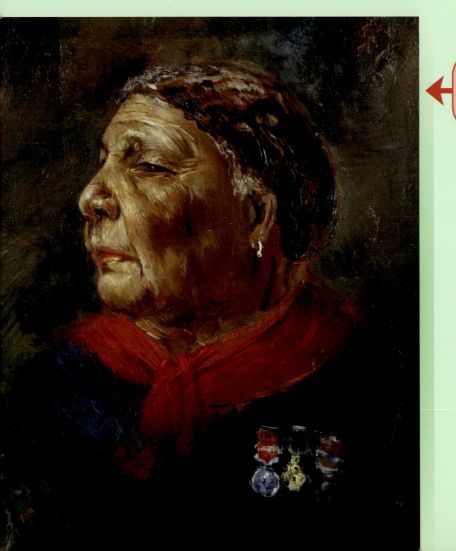

Mary Jane Seacole (n e Grant) Albert Charles Challen, 1869

This portrait of Mary Seacole is very different from the one of Florence Nightingale. Notice that the background has little detail, perhaps because the artist is concentrating on Mary's courageous personality.

Her portrait was painted when she was back in Britain, long after her time nursing in the Crimean War.

The red West Indian scarf around her neck represents the country of her birth and the medals she wears were awarded for her bravery.

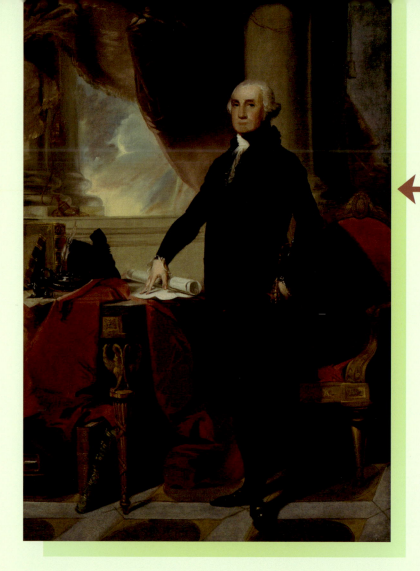

George Washington fought against Britain in the American
War of Independence and became the first President of the
United States of America. His face is famous all over the
world as it appears on the US one-dollar banknote.

J K Rowling is famous for writing the Harry Potter books. She's successful now, but she had very little money before her books made her famous. This portrait isn't a flat painting as the sitter and the objects in the room are cut out and placed in front of the background. The window has light streaming through it, perhaps to show that the author is in an imaginary world in her head, making up stories.

J K Rowling
Stuart Pearson Wright, 2005

Where to see portraits

You can see portraits in art galleries and big houses all over the world. The biggest collection of portraits in a single place is in the National Portrait Gallery in London. There are also National Portrait Galleries in Scotland, Australia, Canada and the United States of America. You can explore their websites to see more portraits.

The National Portrait Gallery, London

The National Portrait Gallery in London tries to make sure everyone gets to share its portraits. Lots of schools come to see them and children also visit with their families.

Children looking at pictures in the National Portrait Gallery, London

You could make your own portrait gallery. Try to put lots of clues into your portraits – use pose, expression, background, clothes and objects – so that people can discover interesting things about your sitters.

Index of pictures

Glossary

arthritis	a condition giving swollen and painful joints
artist's model	someone who is paid to pose for an artist to paint or photograph
background	the setting that is shown behind the main figures in a picture
collage	a picture made up from different materials stuck onto a background
drapes	long pieces of cloth
easel	a stand on which an artist puts a picture while it's being painted
expression	the face that a person makes to show how they're feeling
minarets	tall, narrow towers belonging to Muslim places of worship called mosques
miniature	a very small portrait
mural	a picture painted or drawn directly onto a wall
pose	the position of the body in a portrait
puns	jokes that involve word play
sculptor	an artist who makes three-dimensional works of art
sitter	the person in a portrait
version	a copy of something that is similar to, but not exactly the same as, the original

Clues in portraits

Ideas for guided reading

Learning objectives: appraise a non fiction book for its contents and usefulness by scanning; identify from examples the key features of explanatory texts; prepare for factual research by reviewing what is known, what is needed, what is available and where one might search; respond appropriately to the contributions of others in the light of alternative viewpoints

Curriculum links: Art and design: the roles and purposes of artists, craftspeople and designers; History: Victorian Britain

Interest words: sitters, pose, expression, collage, miniature, sculptor, minarets

Resources: whiteboard, internet, mixed media for making portraits

Getting started

This book may be read over two or more guided reading sessions.

- Read the blurb together and then allow children to browse quickly through book to decide its purpose.

- Decide if the text has the features of an explanation text. Does it answer a question? Are there useful pictures? Is there an introduction? Is it written in the present tense? Are there causal connectives such as *because* and *so*?

- Ask for a selection of volunteers to read aloud pp2–7. Prompt and praise for effective reading including tackling unfamiliar words.

Reading and responding

- Direct the children to read about a portrait independently in preparation for discussing it with others. Observe, prompt and praise as they read.

- Ask each child to introduce their portrait in their own words and discuss what is interesting about it and why they like it.

- Encourage the rest of the group to disagree or agree politely with reasons.